THE WORLD'S WORST NATURAL DISASTERS

THE WORLD'S WORST VOLCANIC ERUPTIONS

by Tracy Nelson Maurer

Raintree is an imprint of Capstone Global Library Limited, a company incorporated in England and Wales having its registered office at 264 Banbury Road, Oxford, OX2 7DY – Registered company number: 6695582

www.raintree.co.uk
myorders@raintree.co.uk

Text © Capstone Global Library Limited 2019
The moral rights of the proprietor have been asserted.

All rights reserved. No part of this publication may be reproduced in any form or by any means (including photocopying or storing it in any medium by electronic means and whether or not transiently or incidentally to some other use of this publication) without the written permission of the copyright owner, except in accordance with the provisions of the Copyright, Designs and Patents Act 1988 or under the terms of a licence issued by the Copyright Licensing Agency, Barnard's Inn, 86 Fetter Lane, London, EC4A 1EN (www.cla.co.uk). Applications for the copyright owner's written permission should be addressed to the publisher.

Edited by Gena Chester
Designed by Juliette Peters
Original illustrations © Capstone Global Library Limited 2019
Picture research by Jo Miller
Production by Tori Abraham
Originated by Capstone Global Library Ltd
Printed and bound in India

ISBN 978 1 4747 7121 4 (hardback)

ISBN 978 1 4747 7125 2 (paperback)

British Library Cataloguing in Publication Data
A full catalogue record for this book is available from the British Library.

Acknowledgements
We would like to thank the following for permission to reproduce photographs: Alamy: FAY 2018, 18–19; AP Images: Pat Roque, 12–13; Bridgeman Images: Private Collection/Look and Learn, 26–27; Dreamstime: George Burba, Cover; Getty Images: Apic/RETIRED/Contributor, 8–9, Langevin Jacques/Contributor, 16–17; Mary Evans Picture Library: Sueddeutsche Zeitung Photo, 10–11; Newscom: VWPics/Francois Gohler, 14–15, ZUMA Press/C. Dan Miller, 20–21; Science Source: Prof. Stewart Lowther, 6–7; Shutterstock: balounm, 24–25, fboudrias, 4–5, leonello calvetti, Cover, 3, 31, peresanz, 22–23, Pete Niesen, 28–29. Design Elements: Shutterstock: fboudrias, Ivana Milic, xpixel.

Every effort has been made to contact copyright holders of material reproduced in this book. Any omissions will be rectified in subsequent printings if notice is given to the publisher.

All the internet addresses (URLs) given in this book were valid at the time of going to press. However, due to the dynamic nature of the internet, some addresses may have changed, or sites may have changed or ceased to exist since publication. While the author and publisher regret any inconvenience this may cause readers, no responsibility for any such changes can be accepted by either the author or the publisher.

CONTENTS

Ready to blow! 4
How volcanoes erupt 6
Deadliest 20th-century eruption 8
Record breaker 10
Amazing evacuations 12
Hot Hawaiian topic 14
Killer river 16
South America's worst volcano 18
Deadly eruption in the USA 20
Supervolcano countdown 22
Buried for centuries 24
What's that sound? 26
Stay away 28

Glossary 30
Find out more 31
Comprehension questions 32
Index 32

READY TO BLOW!

Earthquakes shake the ground. The air smells like rotten eggs. Steam pours from the top of a nearby mountain. This isn't just any mountain. It's a volcano ready to **erupt**!

VEI SCALE

Scientists use the Volcanic Explosivity Index (VEI) to measure an eruption. Each eruption is rated from 0 (small) to 8 (huge).

VEI:
0
1
2
3
4
5
6
7
8

FACT Earth's last VEI 8 happened about 27,000 years ago in New Zealand.

erupt burst out suddenly with great force

HOW VOLCANOES ERUPT

Some volcanoes erupt slowly. **Magma** oozes out and gives people time to escape. Other volcanoes have explosive eruptions. Magma rumbles deep beneath the earth. Then earthquakes shake the magma, like fizzy drink in a bottle. The pressure sends **lava**, **toxic** gas and ash out of the volcano.

magma melted rock found beneath Earth's surface
lava hot, liquid rock that pours out of a volcano when it erupts
toxic poisonous

DEADLIEST 20TH-CENTURY ERUPTION

Location:
Mount Pelée, Martinique

Date:
8 May 1902

VEI: 4

0
1
2
3
4 ◀
5
6
7
8

Mount Pelée's eruption in 1902 destroyed the town of St. Pierre, Martinique. Deadly gas and ash rushed down the volcano's peak at about 160 kilometres (100 miles) per hour. Almost 30,000 people died.

FACT On 7 May, a volcano on an island near Mount Pelée also erupted. It killed 1,500 people.

RECORD BREAKER

Location:
Mount Tambora, Indonesia

Date:
5–10 April 1815

VEI: 7

0
1
2
3
4
5
6
7
8

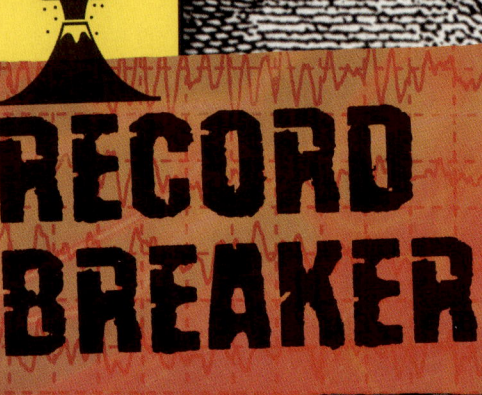

10

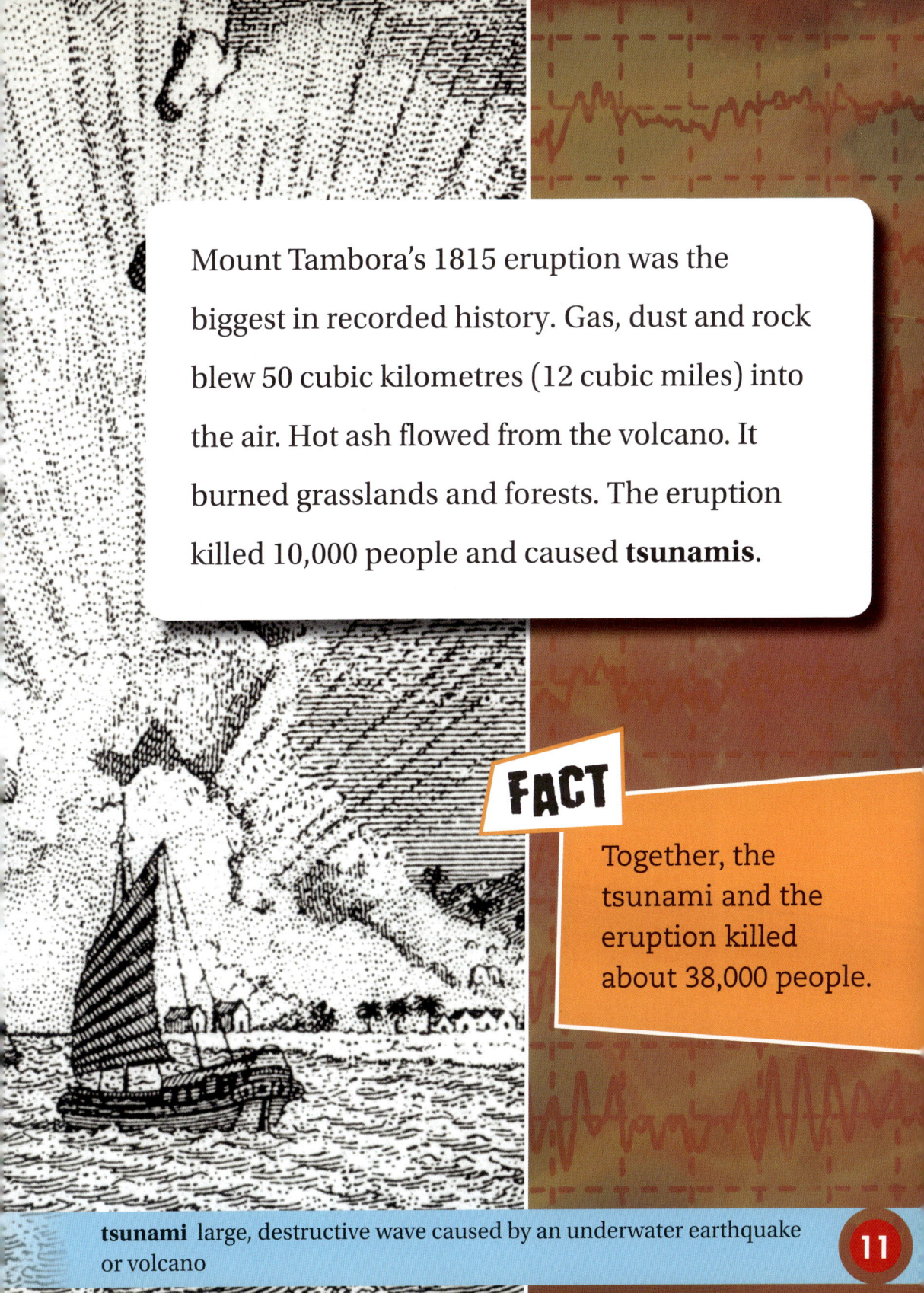

Mount Tambora's 1815 eruption was the biggest in recorded history. Gas, dust and rock blew 50 cubic kilometres (12 cubic miles) into the air. Hot ash flowed from the volcano. It burned grasslands and forests. The eruption killed 10,000 people and caused **tsunamis**.

FACT

Together, the tsunami and the eruption killed about 38,000 people.

tsunami large, destructive wave caused by an underwater earthquake or volcano

AMAZING EVACUATIONS

Location:
Mount Pinatubo, Philippines

Date:
15 June 1991

VEI: 6

0
1
2
3
4
5
6
7
8

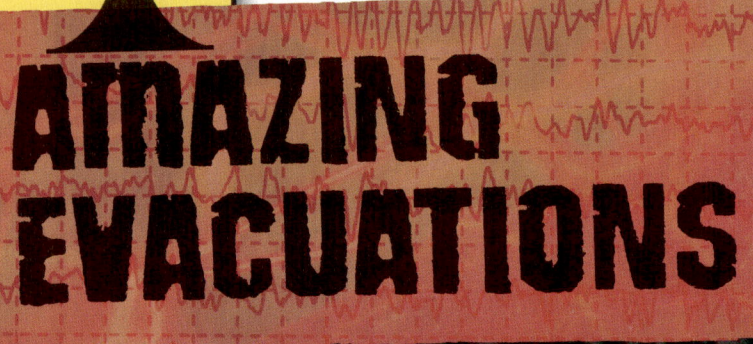

FACT

Mount Pinatubo spread ash for 35 kilometres (22 miles). It reached neighbouring villages and the US Clark Air Base.

Modern science saved lives when Mount Pinatubo erupted in 1991. Scientists saw the warning signs that the volcano was about to blow. They told people to **evacuate**. As many as 20,000 people listened. Even so, about 300 people lost their lives.

evacuate leave an area during a time of danger

HOT HAWAIIAN TOPIC

Location:
Kilauea Volcano, the Big Island of Hawaii, USA

Date:
3 May 2018

VEI: 1

0
1 ◀
2
3
4
5
6
7
8

The world's most active volcano is Kilauea. Hot lava has oozed from it since 1983. On 3 May 2018, new openings in the ground created fresh paths for lava flow. No one knows when the eruption will end.

FACT

Volcanoes made each of the Hawaiian Islands. Only the volcanoes Kilauea and Mauna Loa are still active.

KILLER RIVER

Location:
Nevado del Ruiz Volcano, Colombia

Date:
13 November 1985

VEI: 3

0
1
2
3 ◀
4
5
6
7
8

The Nevado del Ruiz Volcano erupted in 1985. Heat from the eruption melted mountain snow and ice. The water mixed with volcanic ash and mud. It flooded the town of Armero. About 25,000 people died.

FACT

Most of the world's volcanoes border the Pacific Ocean. This area of volcanoes and earthquake activity is called "The Ring of Fire".

SOUTH AMERICA'S WORST VOLCANO

Location:
Huaynaputina Volcano, Peru

Date:
19 February 1600

VEI: 6

0
1
2
3
4
5
6 ◁
7
8

Huaynaputina surprised everyone when the powerful volcano erupted in 1600. Hot mudflows reached the Pacific Ocean, 120 kilometres (75 miles) away. It is the largest known eruption in South America.

Deadly Eruption in the USA

Location: Mount St. Helens, Washington, USA

Date: 18 May 1980

VEI: 5

0
1
2
3
4
5
6
7
8

Mount St. Helens erupted in a big way in 1980. The north side of the mountain blew off! It caused a massive **landslide**. The eruption killed 57 people.

FACT

The air blast from Mount St. Helens' eruption tore down trees within 518 square kilometres (200 square miles).

landslide large mass of earth and rocks that suddenly slides down a mountain or hill

SUPERVOLCANO COUNTDOWN

Location:
Yellowstone National Park, Wyoming, USA

Date:
640,000 years ago

VEI: 8

0
1
2
3
4
5
6
7
8 ◀

Yellowstone National Park in the United States has had three VEI 8 eruptions. The last one was 640,000 years ago. If the supervolcano were to erupt again, ash could reach as far as the Atlantic Ocean. Scientists watch for signs of another big eruption to help warn people in time.

FACT The magma underneath Yellowstone could fill the Grand Canyon 11 times.

BURIED FOR CENTURIES

Location:
Mount Vesuvius, Italy

Date:
24 August 79 AD

VEI: 5

0
1
2
3
4
5 ◂
6
7
8

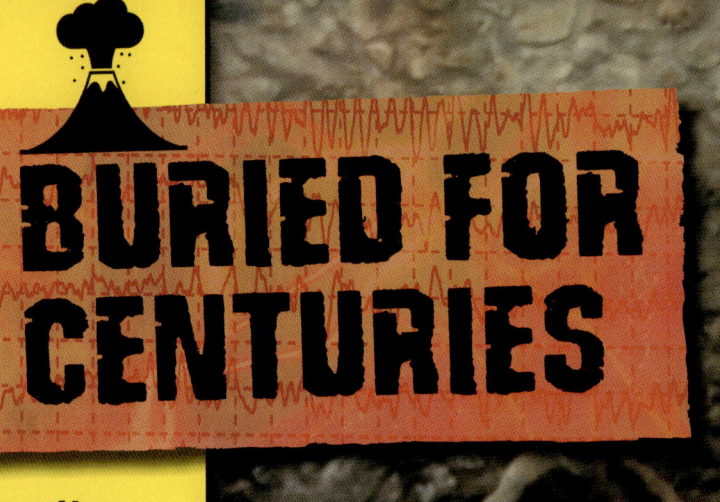

Almost 2,000 years ago, Mount Vesuvius gushed hot ash, rock and toxic gas. The hot volcanic flow killed people instantly in the cities of Pompeii and Herculaneum. Their bodies were **preserved** in volcanic ash until they were discovered about 1700 years later.

FACT

A man called Pliny the Younger saw Vesuvius erupt. He later wrote down what he saw. Today the biggest and most powerful type of eruption, **plinian**, is named after him.

preserved something that has stayed in its original condition

plinian large volcanic eruption in which gas, ash and volcanic rock is sent high into the air

WHAT'S THAT SOUND?

Location:
Krakatoa, Indonesia

Date:
26 August 1883

VEI: 6

0
1
2
3
4
5
6 ◀
7
8

Multiple explosions rocked the island of Krakatoa in 1883. They were heard up to 3,500 kilometres (2,200 miles) away. Only a few people died from the eruption. But the blasts also set off tsunamis, which hit many nearby islands. Around 36,000 people drowned.

FACT

The ash from the eruption completely covered Krakatoa. It took five years for plant and animal life to fully return to the island.

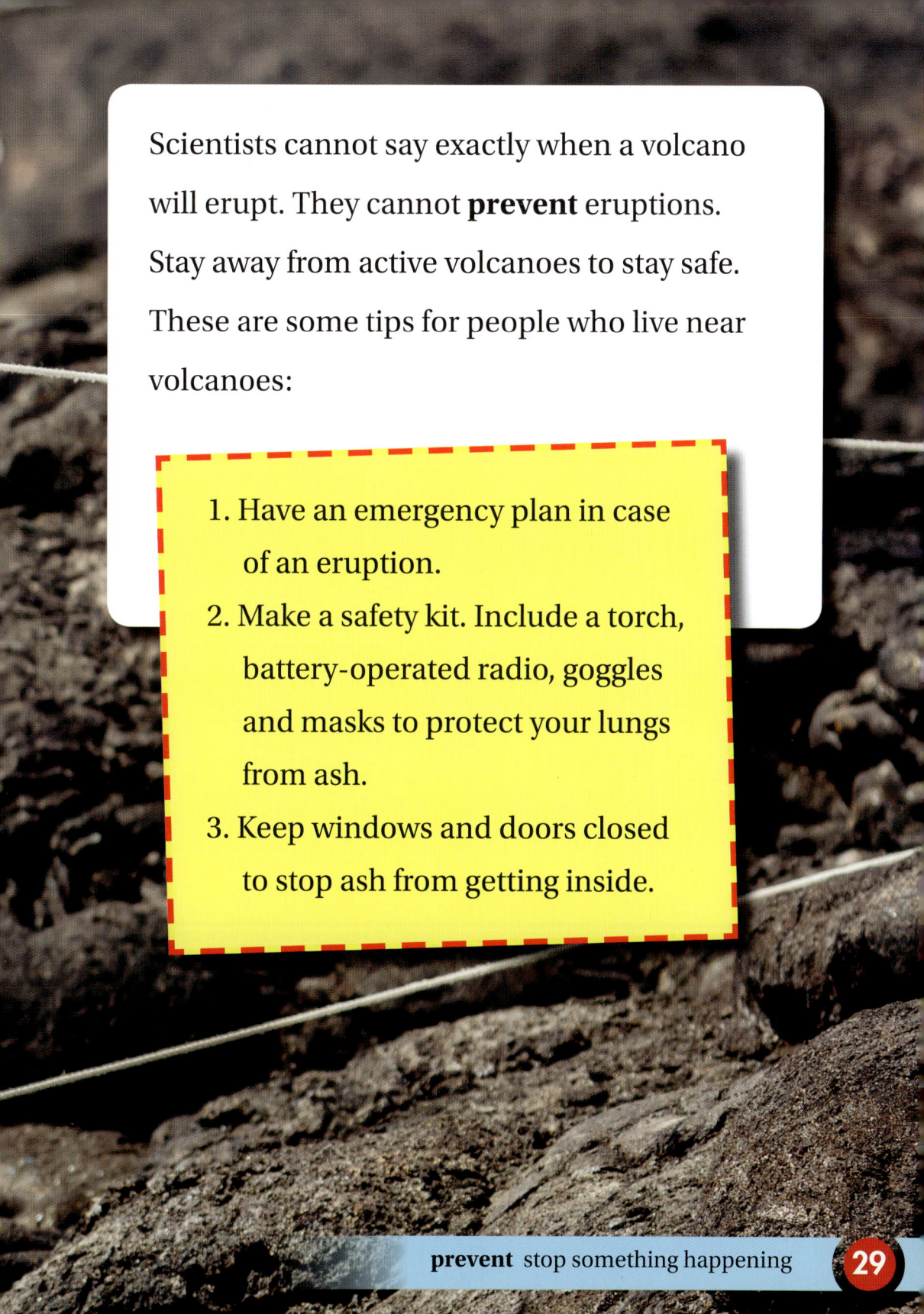

Scientists cannot say exactly when a volcano will erupt. They cannot **prevent** eruptions. Stay away from active volcanoes to stay safe. These are some tips for people who live near volcanoes:

1. Have an emergency plan in case of an eruption.
2. Make a safety kit. Include a torch, battery-operated radio, goggles and masks to protect your lungs from ash.
3. Keep windows and doors closed to stop ash from getting inside.

prevent stop something happening

GLOSSARY

erupt burst out suddenly with great force

evacuate leave an area during a time of danger

landslide large mass of earth and rocks that suddenly slides down a mountain or hill

lava hot, liquid rock that pours out of a volcano when it erupts

magma melted rock found beneath Earth's surface

plinian large volcanic eruption in which gas, ash and volcanic rock is sent high into the air

preserved something that has stayed in its original condition

prevent stop something happening

toxic poisonous

tsunami large, destructive wave caused by an underwater earthquake or volcano

FIND OUT MORE

BOOKS

How Does a Volcano Become an Island (How Does It Happen), Linda Tagliaferro (Raintree, 2016)

Science vs Natural Disasters (Science Fights Back), Angela Royston (Raintree, 2016)

Volcanoes (DKfindout!), DK (DK Children, 2016)

Volcanologist (The Coolest Jobs on the Planet), Hugh Tuffen and Melanie Waldron (Raintree, 2015)

WEBSITES

www.bbc.co.uk/programmes/p006vjjv
Learn more about volcanoes and volcanic eruptions.

www.dkfindout.com/uk/gallery/history/objects-found-at-pompeii
Look at some of the preserved remains at Pompeii.

Comprehension Questions

1. How do volcanoes erupt?

2. When volcanic ash in the air blocks the sun for weeks, what might happen to the temperature? What might happen to plant life?

3. What is an eruption called when ash, gas and volcanic rock are sent high into the air?

Index

ash 6, 8, 11, 13, 16, 22, 25, 27, 29

Atlantic Ocean 22

earthquakes 4, 6

gas 6, 8, 11, 25

lava 6, 14

magma 6

Pacific Ocean 19

rocks 11, 25

scientists 13, 22, 29

South America 19

supervolcanoes 22

tsunamis 11, 27